Mandala
TRIP

CHAPTER · I

I

Artist's name

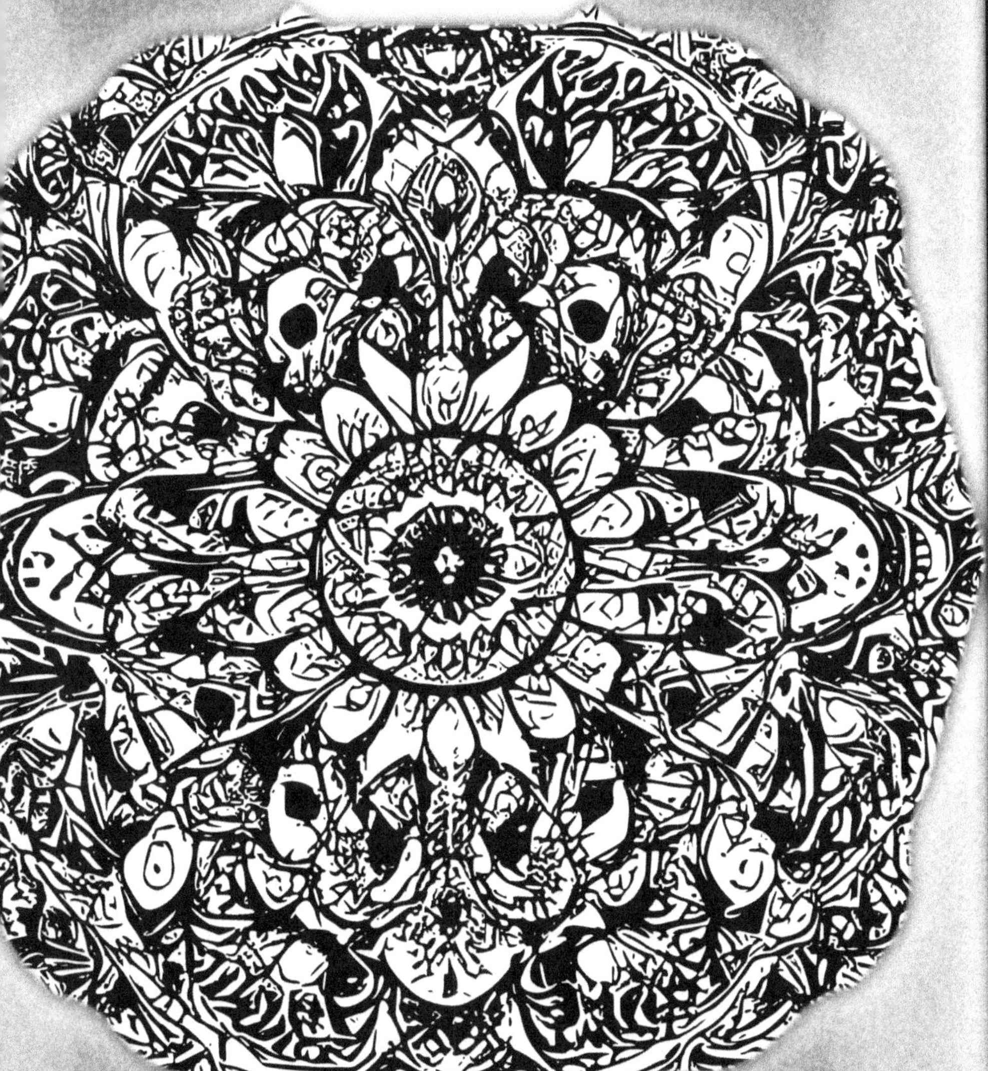

Date

Mandala
TRIP

CHAPTER 1

II

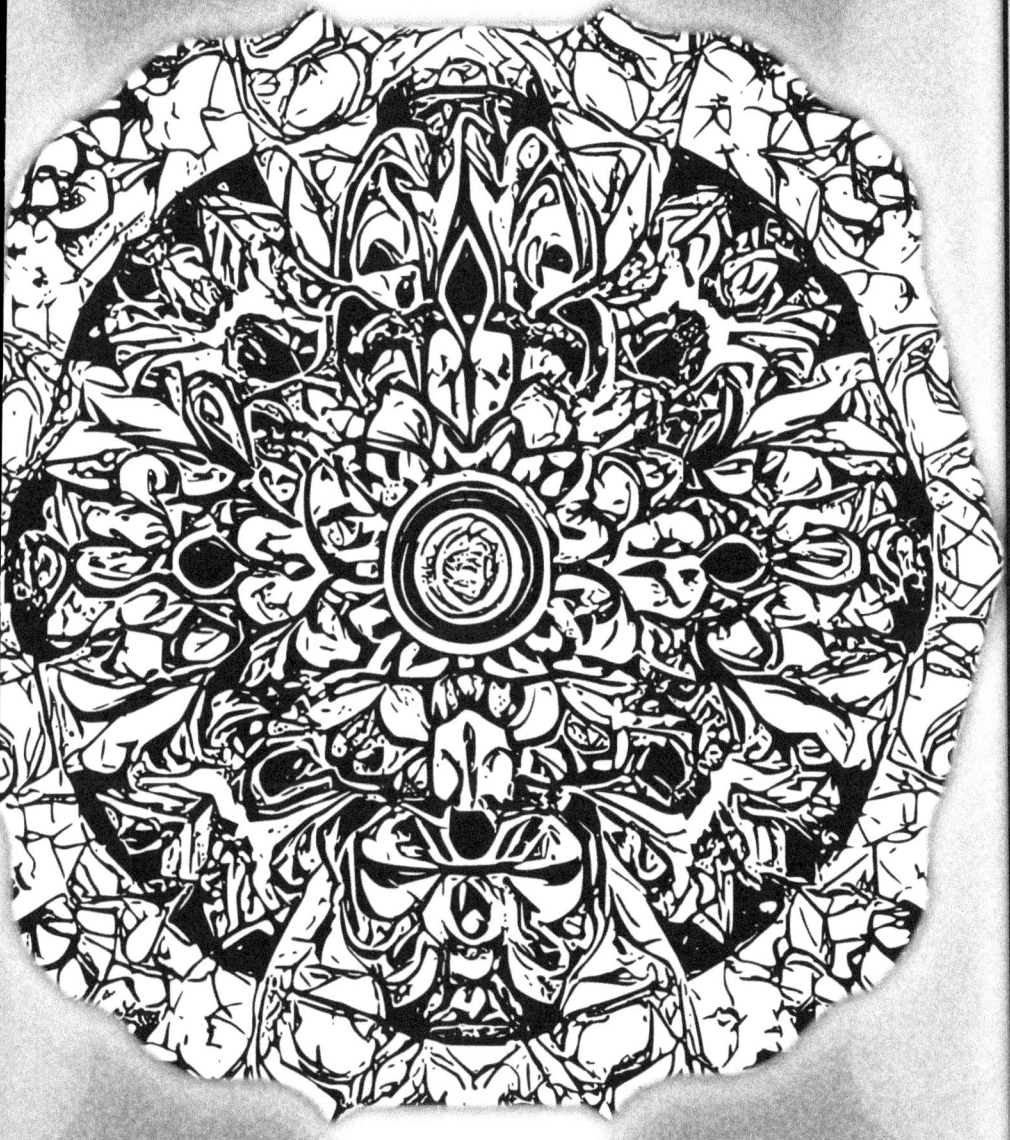

Artist's name

Date

Mandala
TRIP

CHAPTER - I

III

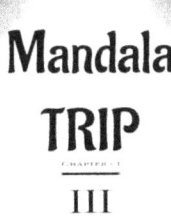

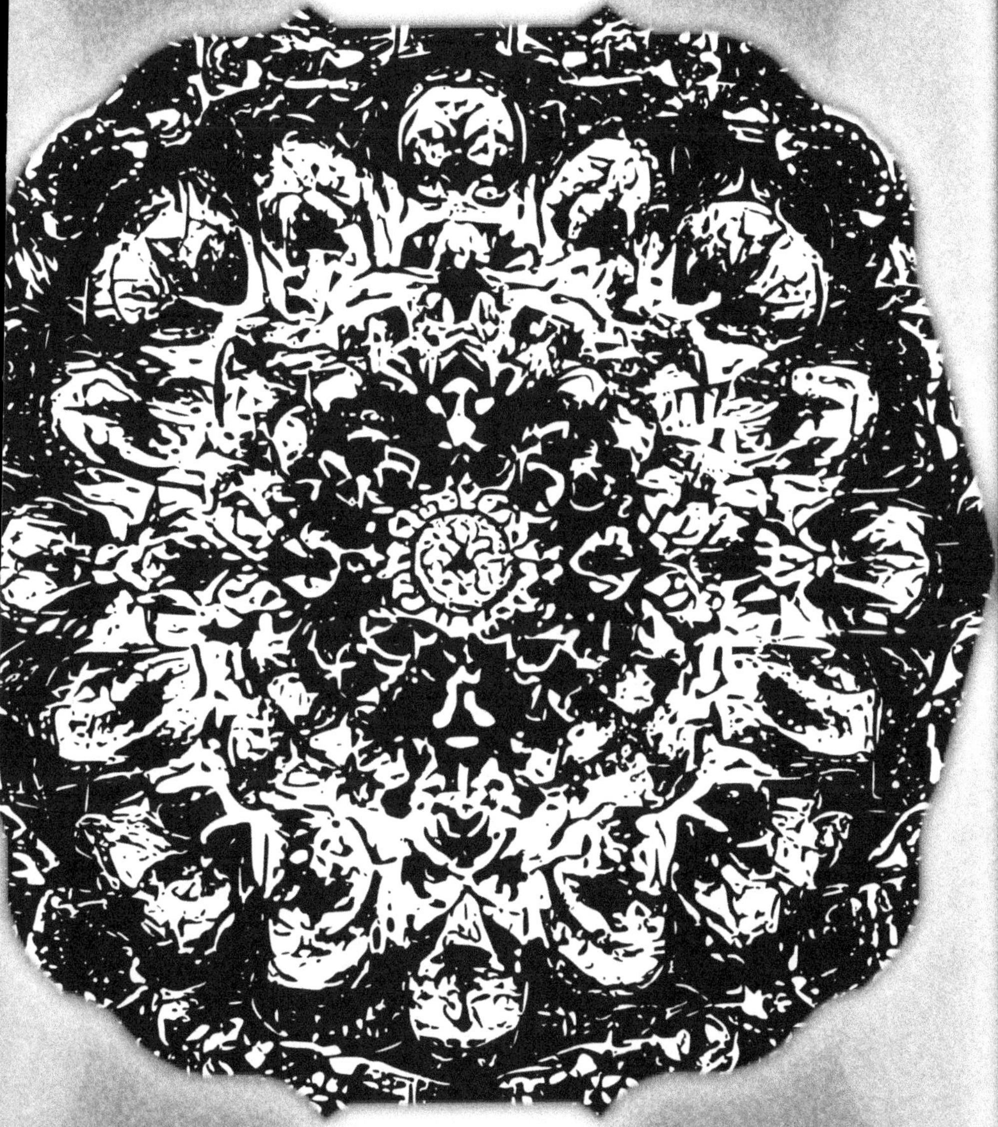

Artist's name

Date

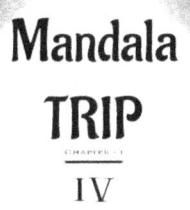

Mandala
TRIP
CHAPTER · I
IV

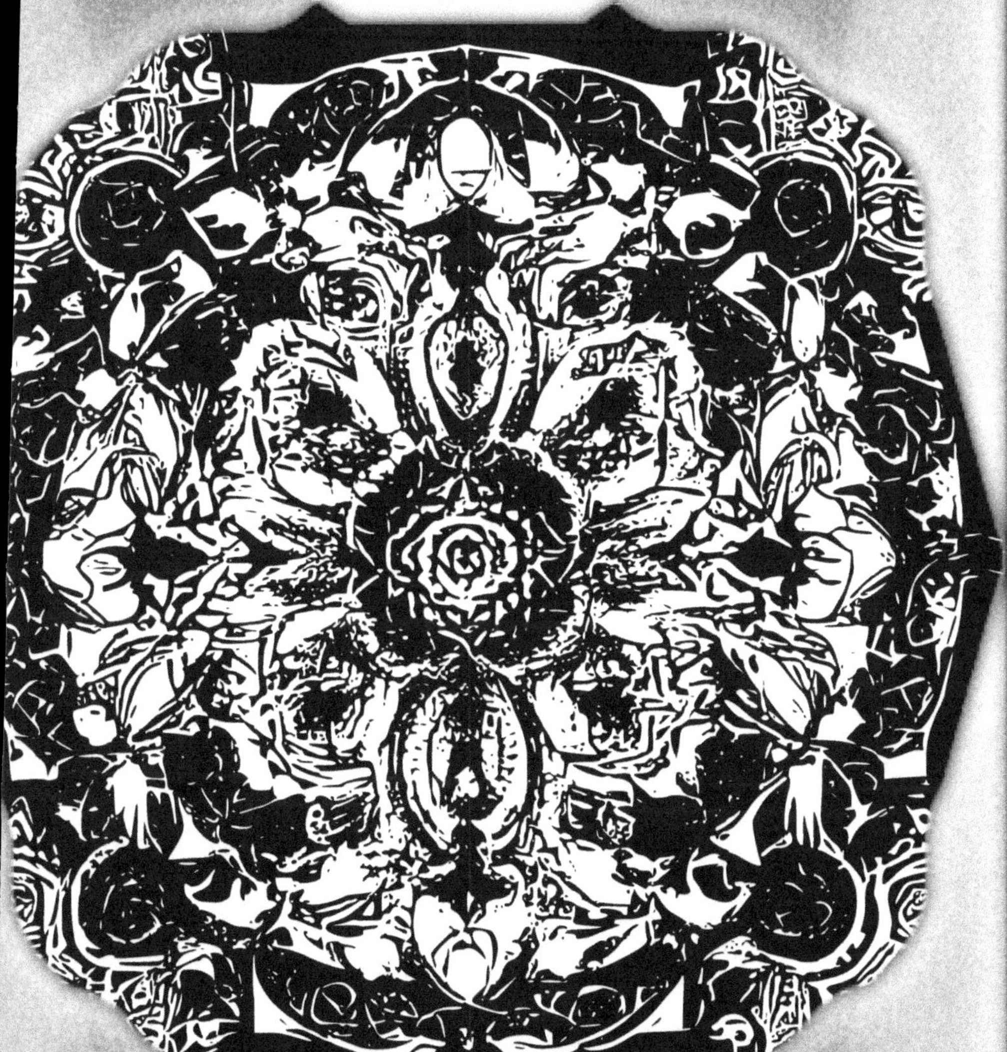

Artist's name

Date

Mandala
TRIP
CHAPTER V
V

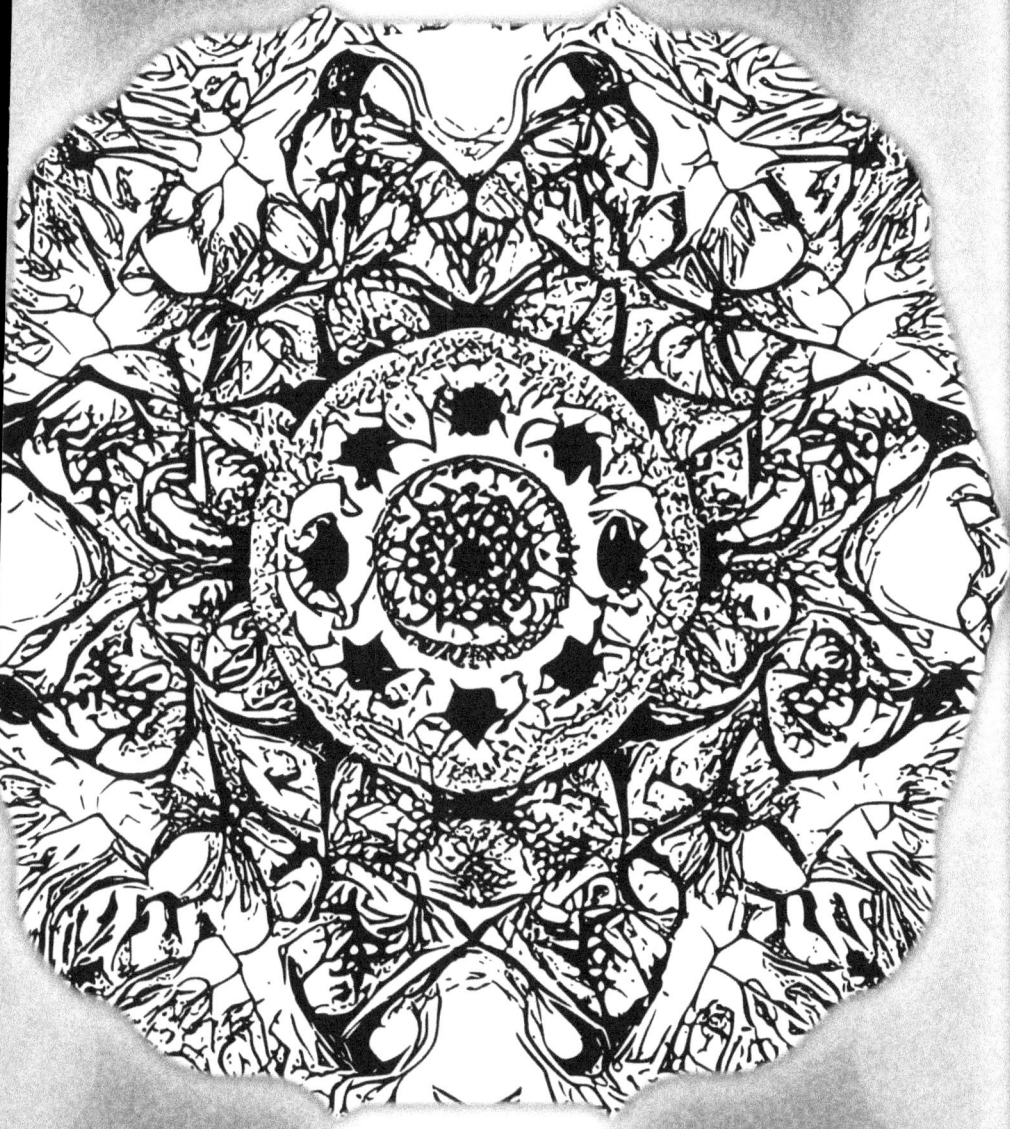

Artist's name

Date

Mandala

TRIP

CHAPTER · 1

VI

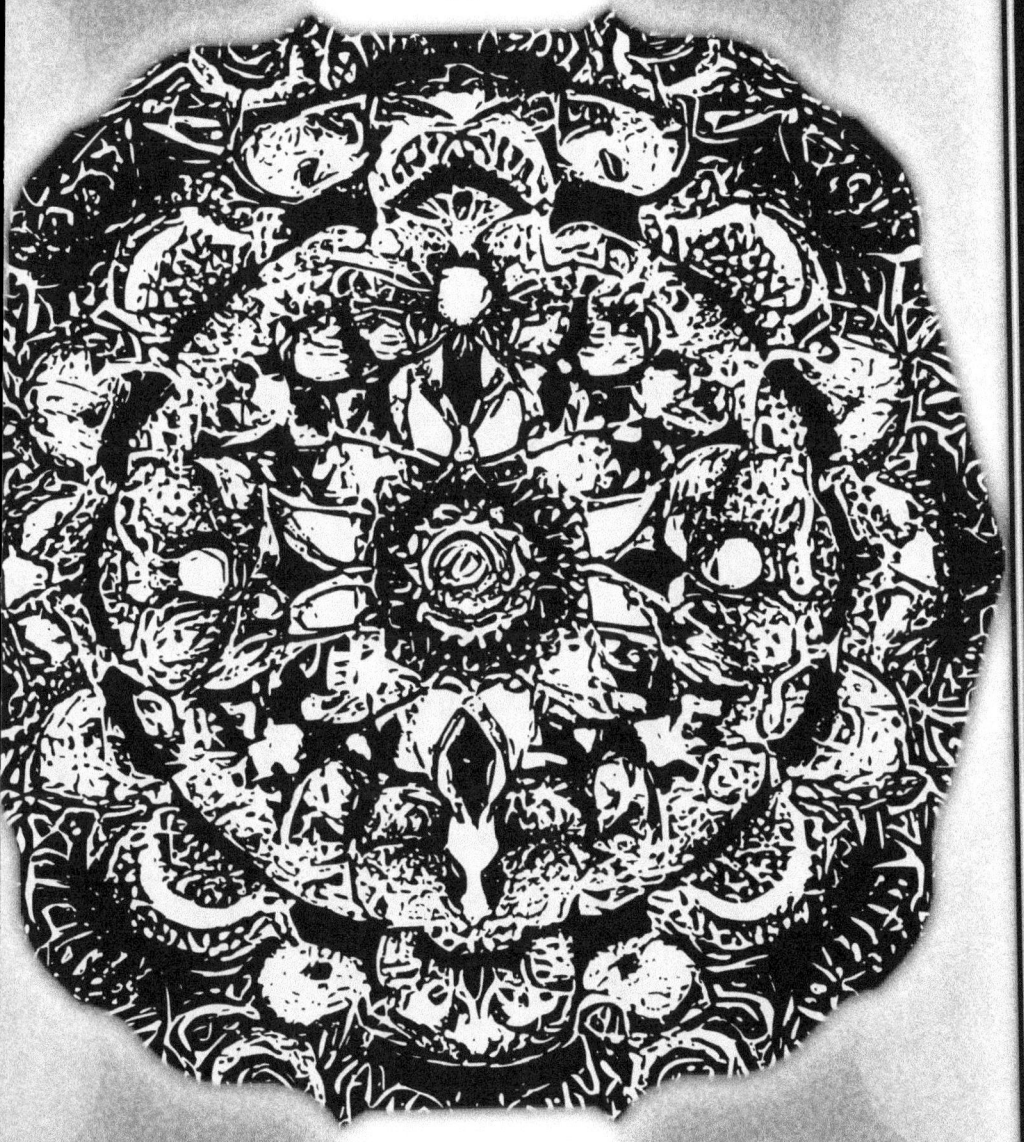

_____

Artist's name

_____

Date

Mandala

TRIP

CHAPTER - 1

VII

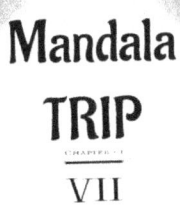

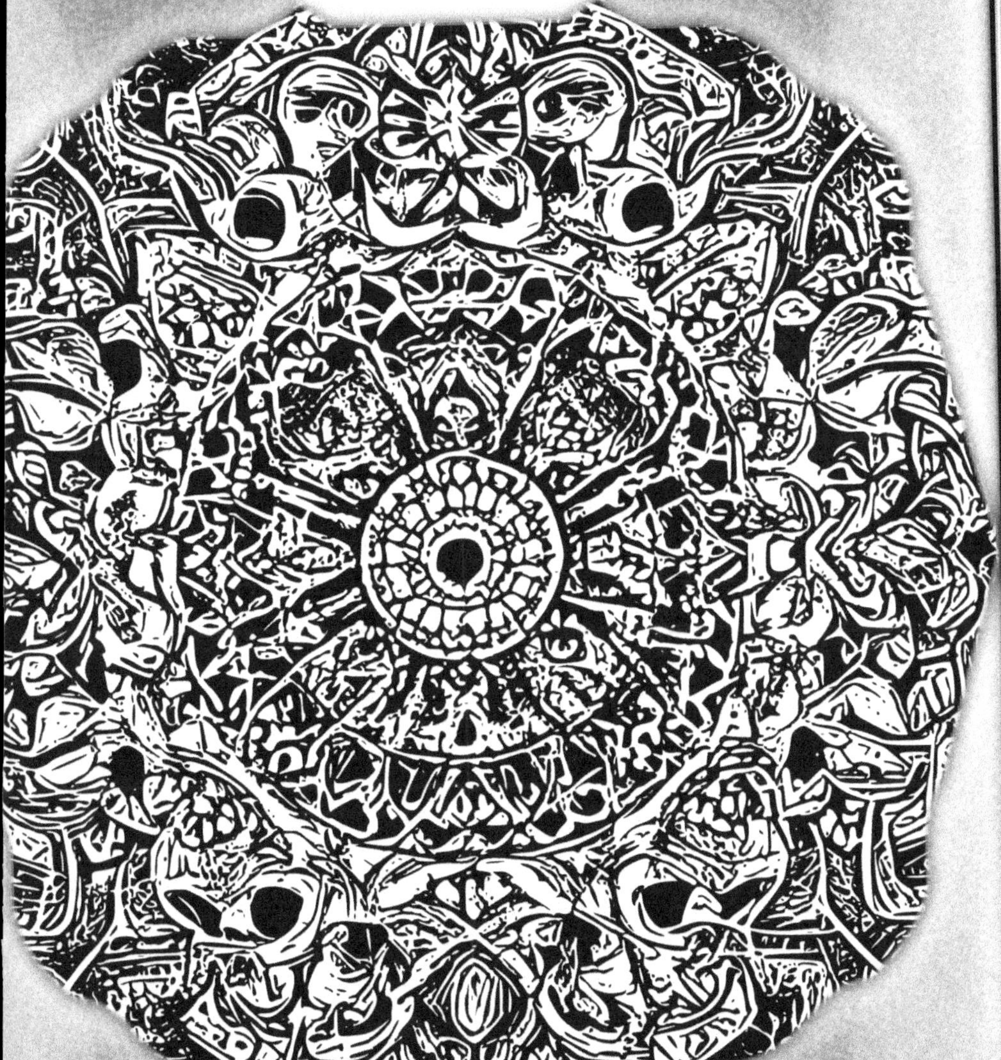

Artist's name

Date

Mandala
TRIP
CHAPTER·1
VIII

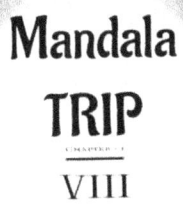

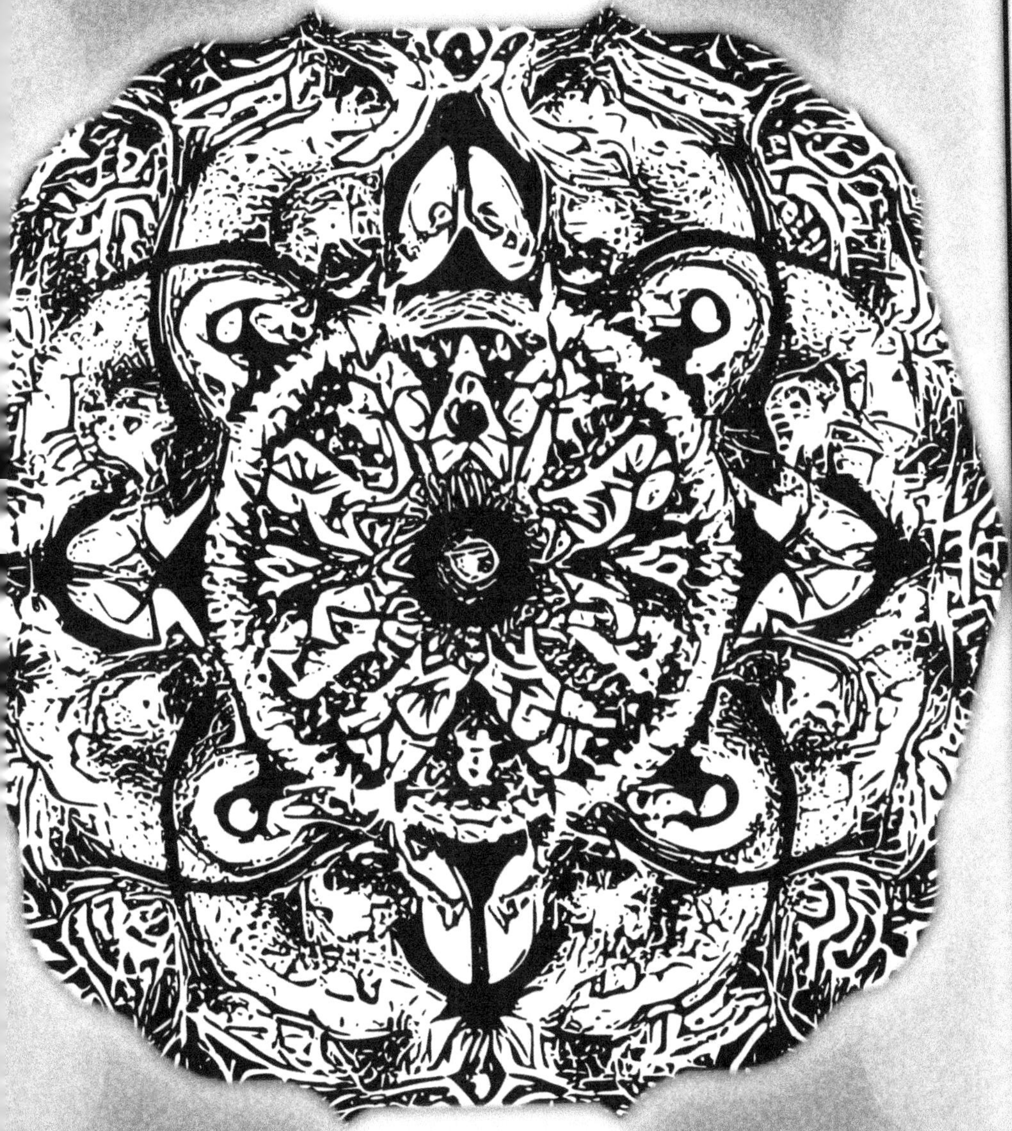

Artist's name

Date

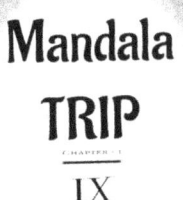

Mandala
TRIP
CHAPTER - 1
IX

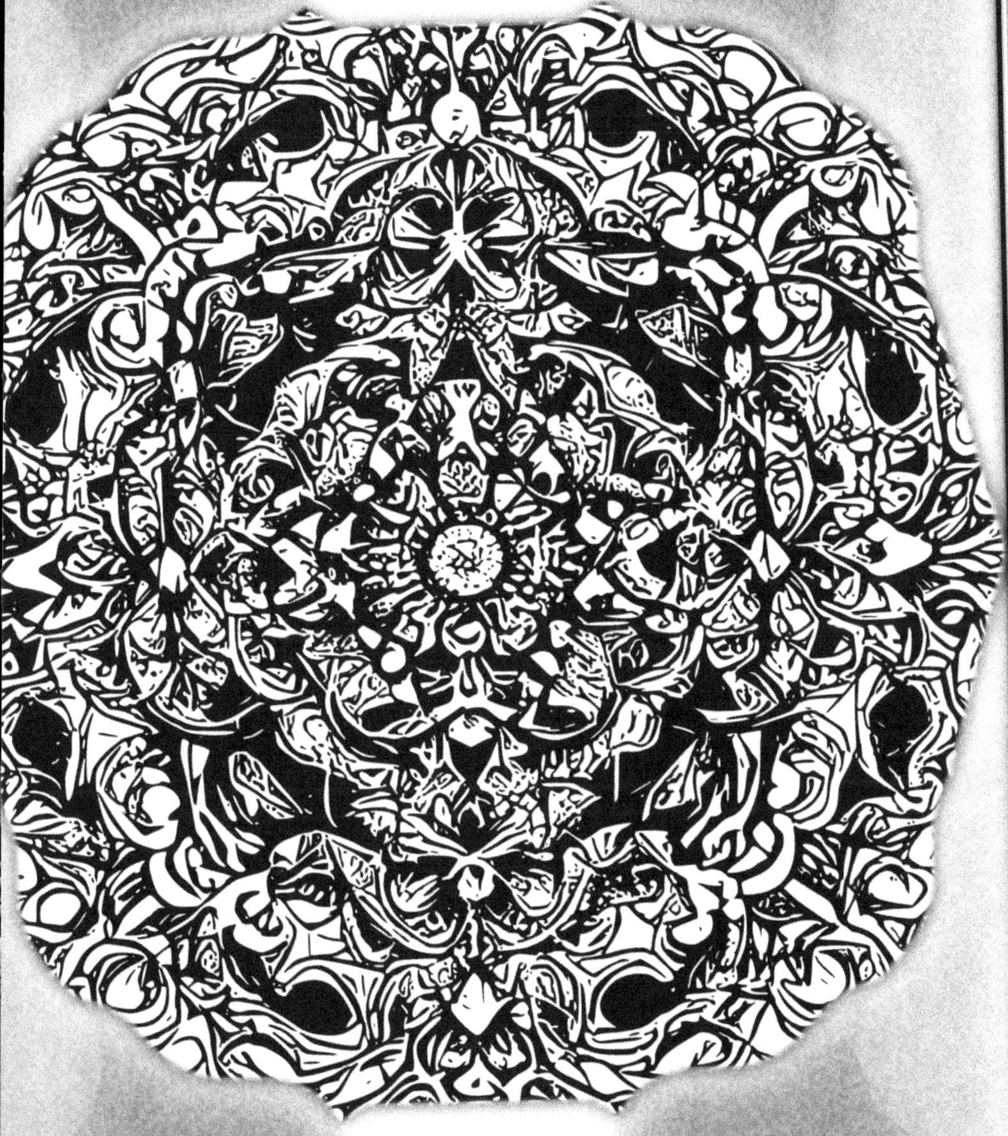

Artist's name

Date

Mandala
TRIP

CHAPTER · 1

X

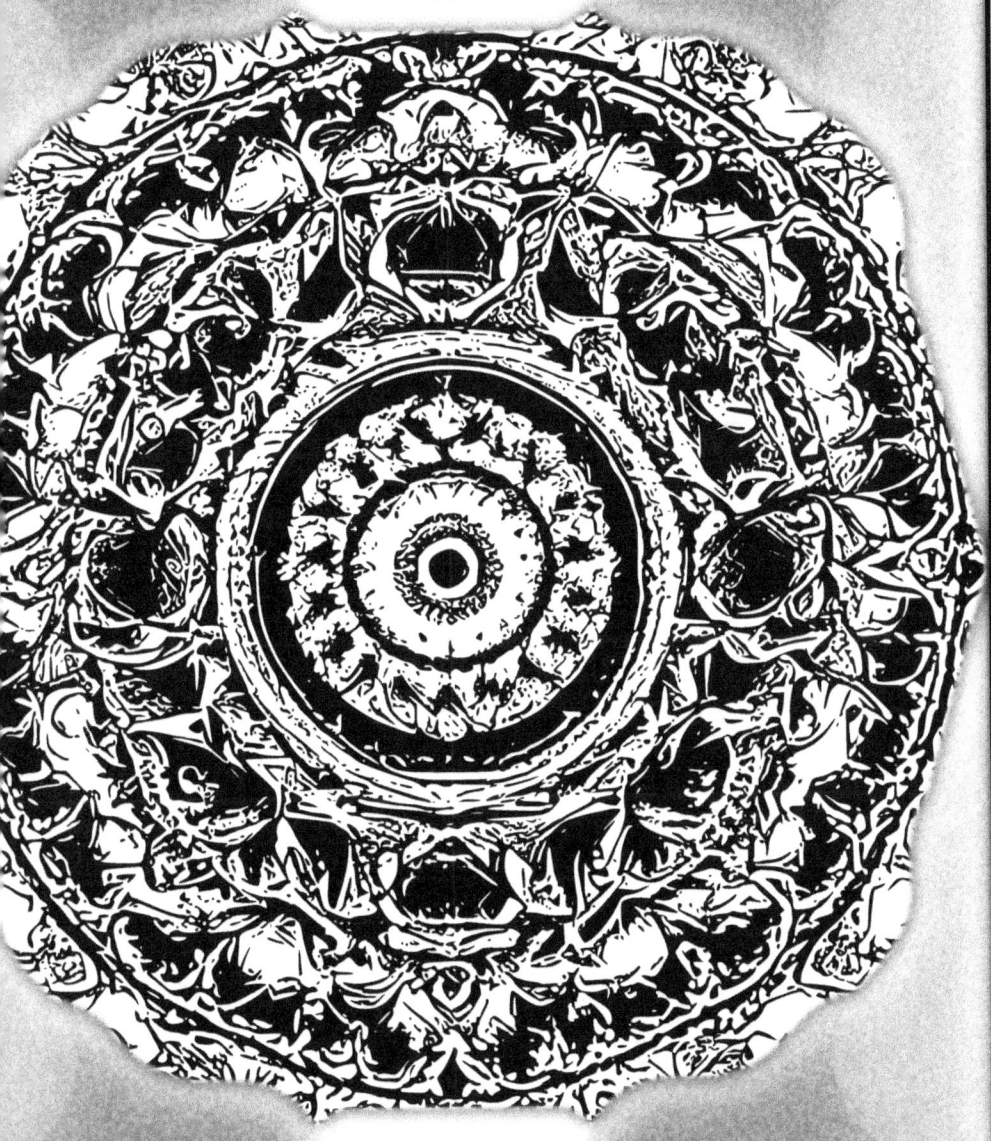

Artist's name

Date

Mandala
TRIP
CHAPTER 1
XI

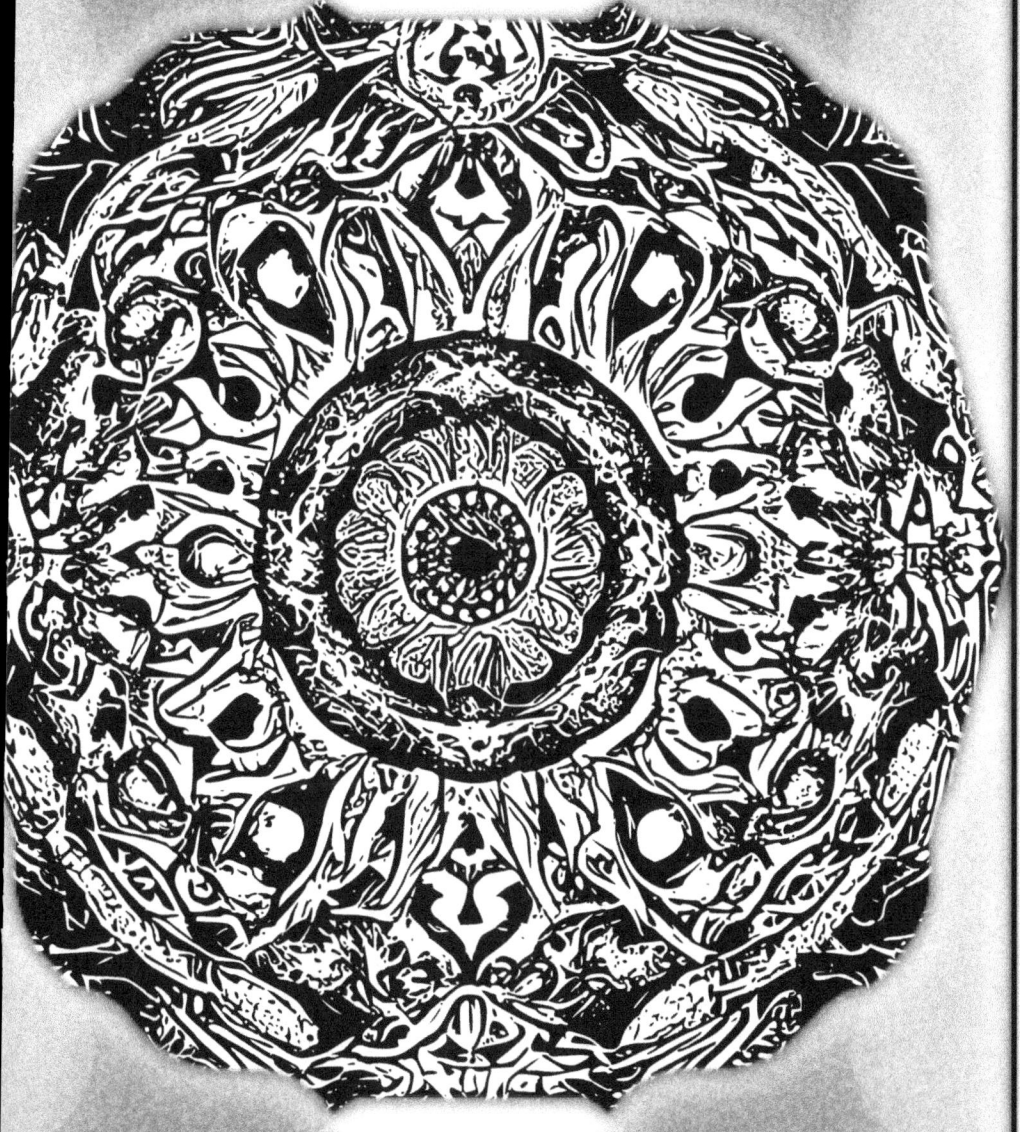

Artist's name

Date

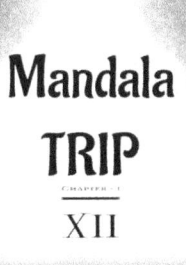

Mandala
TRIP

CHAPTER - 1

XII

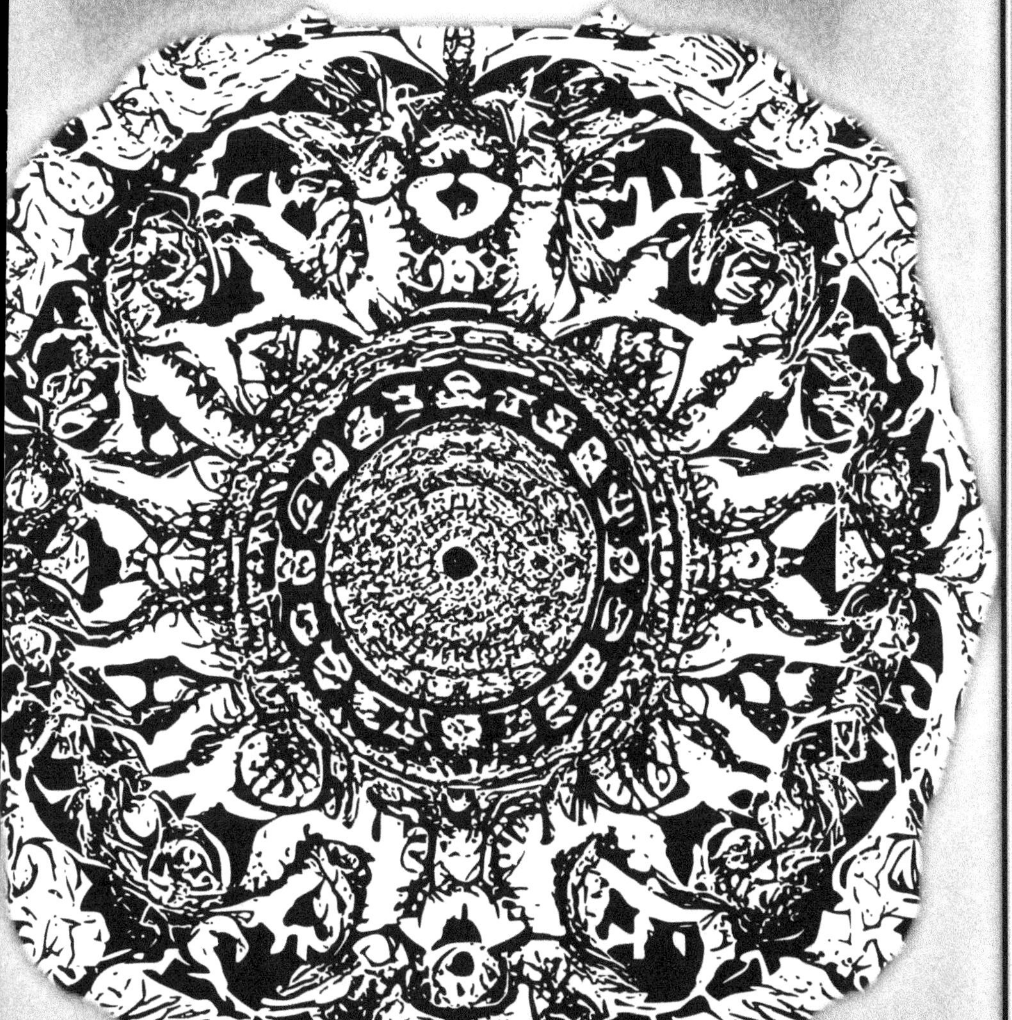

_____

Artist's name

_____

Date

Mandala

TRIP

CHAPTER · 1

XIII

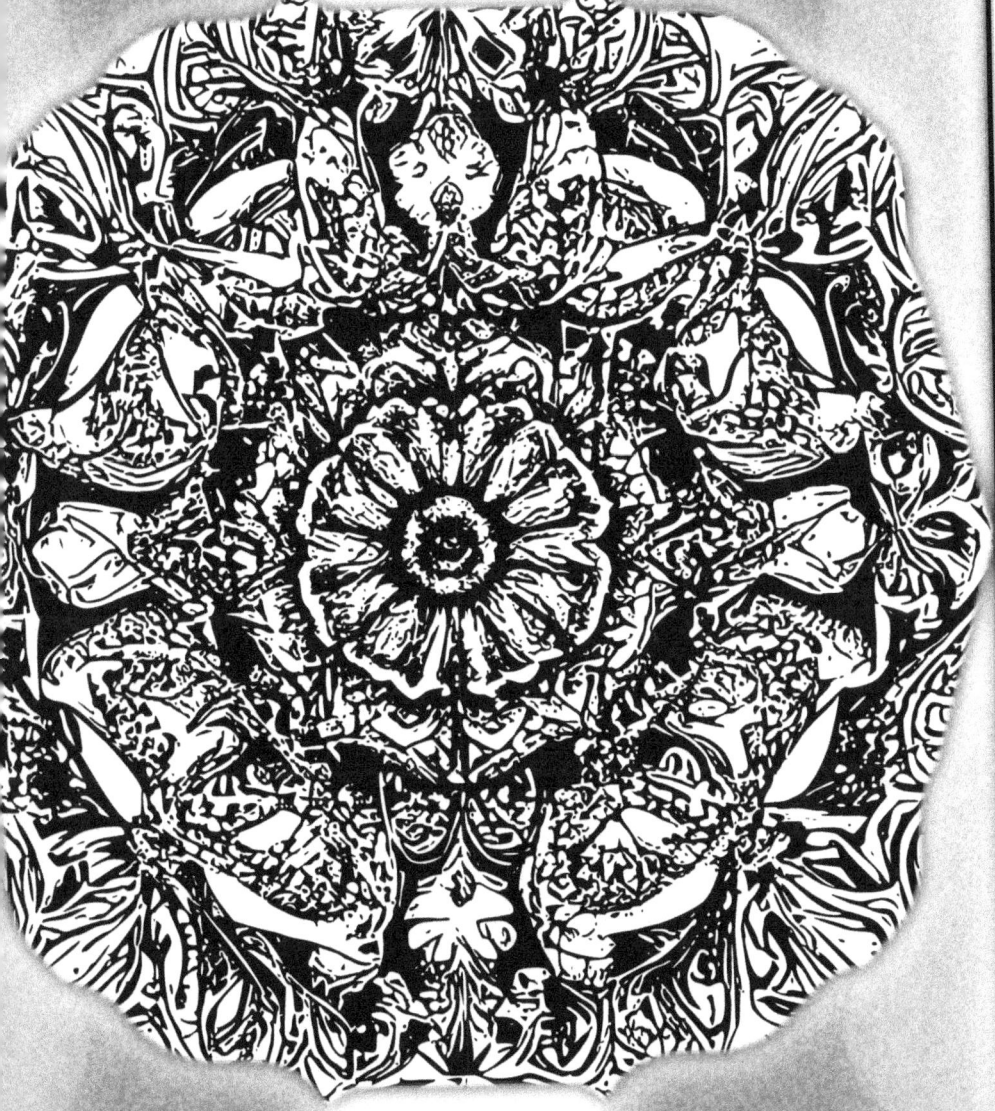

Artist's name

Date

Mandala

TRIP
CHAPTER 1

XIV

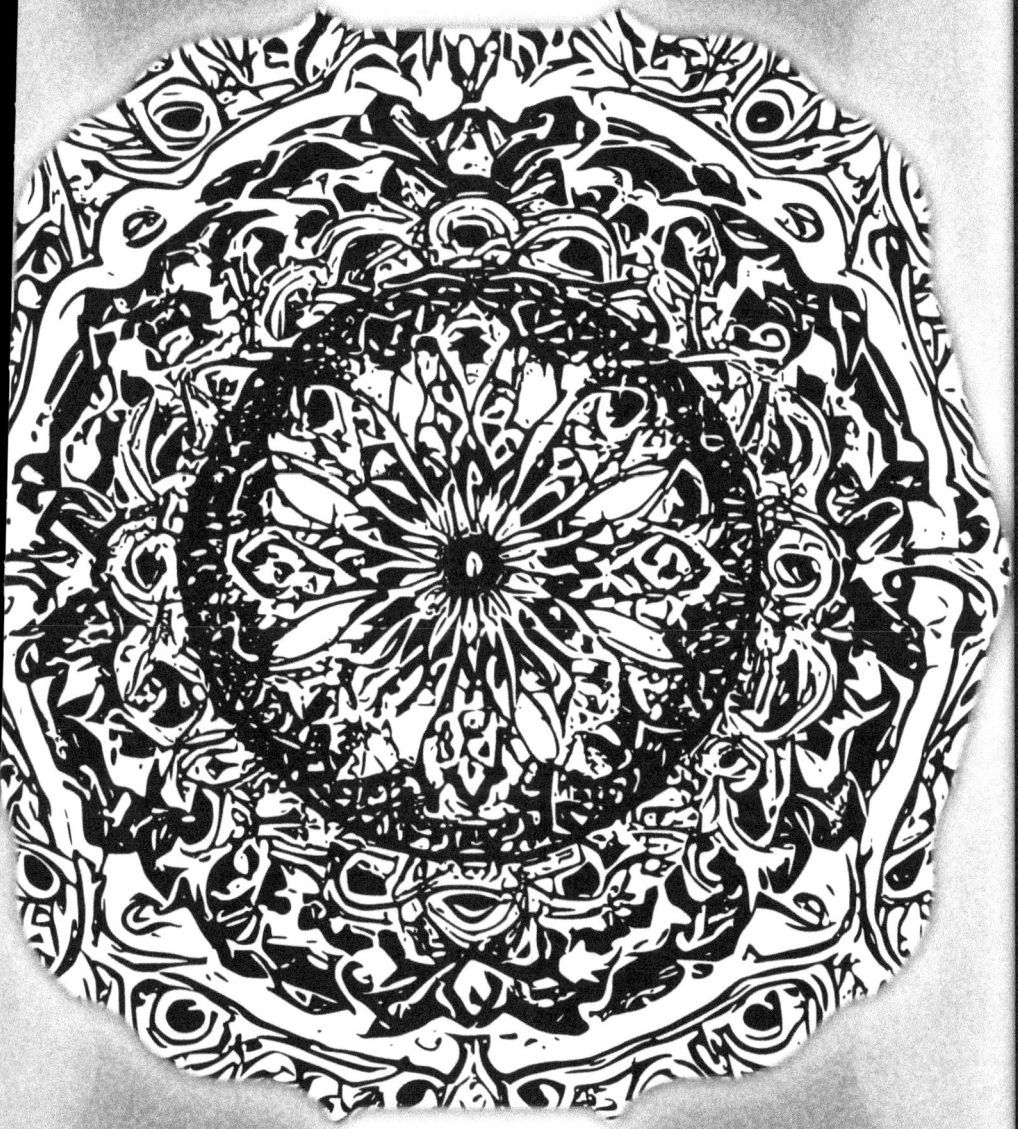

Artist's name

Date

Mandala
TRIP
CHAPTER · 1
XV

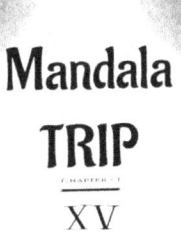

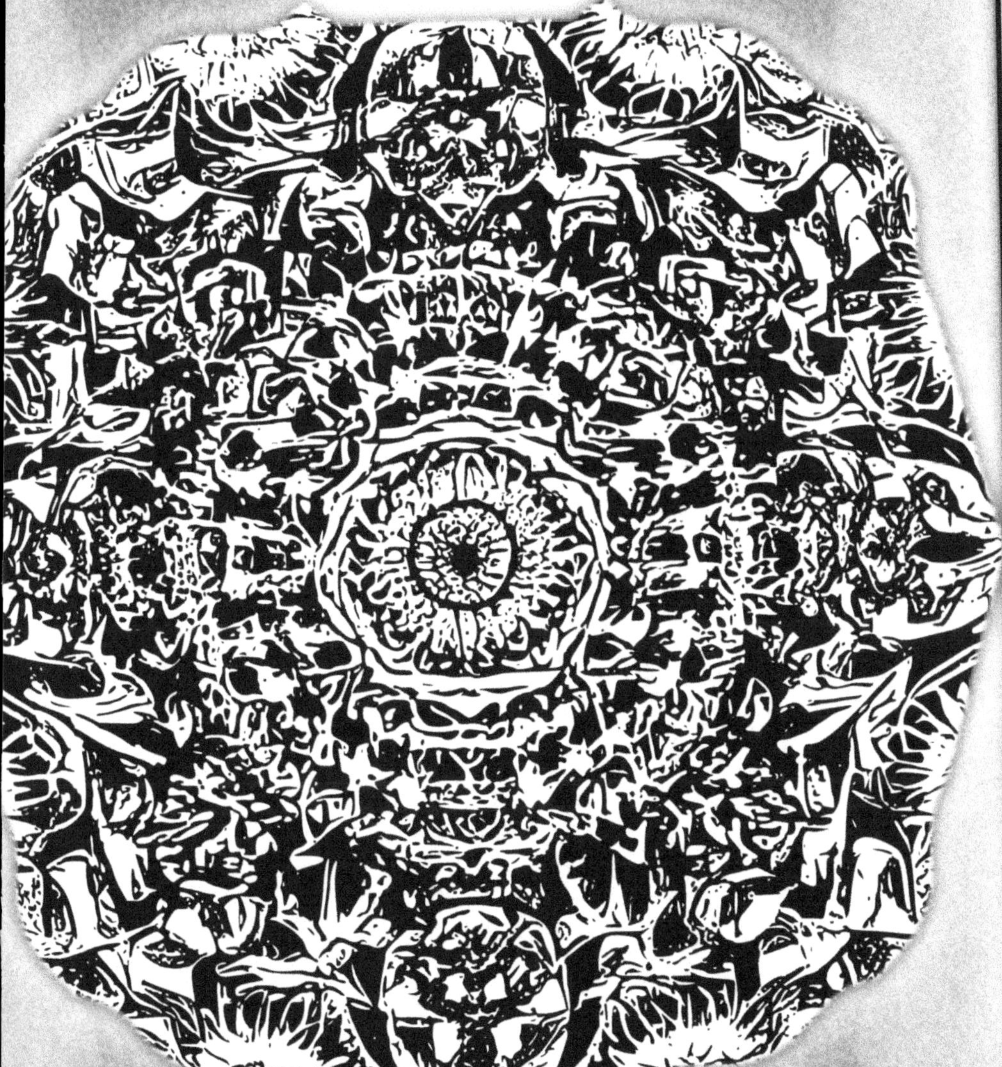

Artist's name

Date

Mandala
TRIP
CHAPTER - 1

XVI

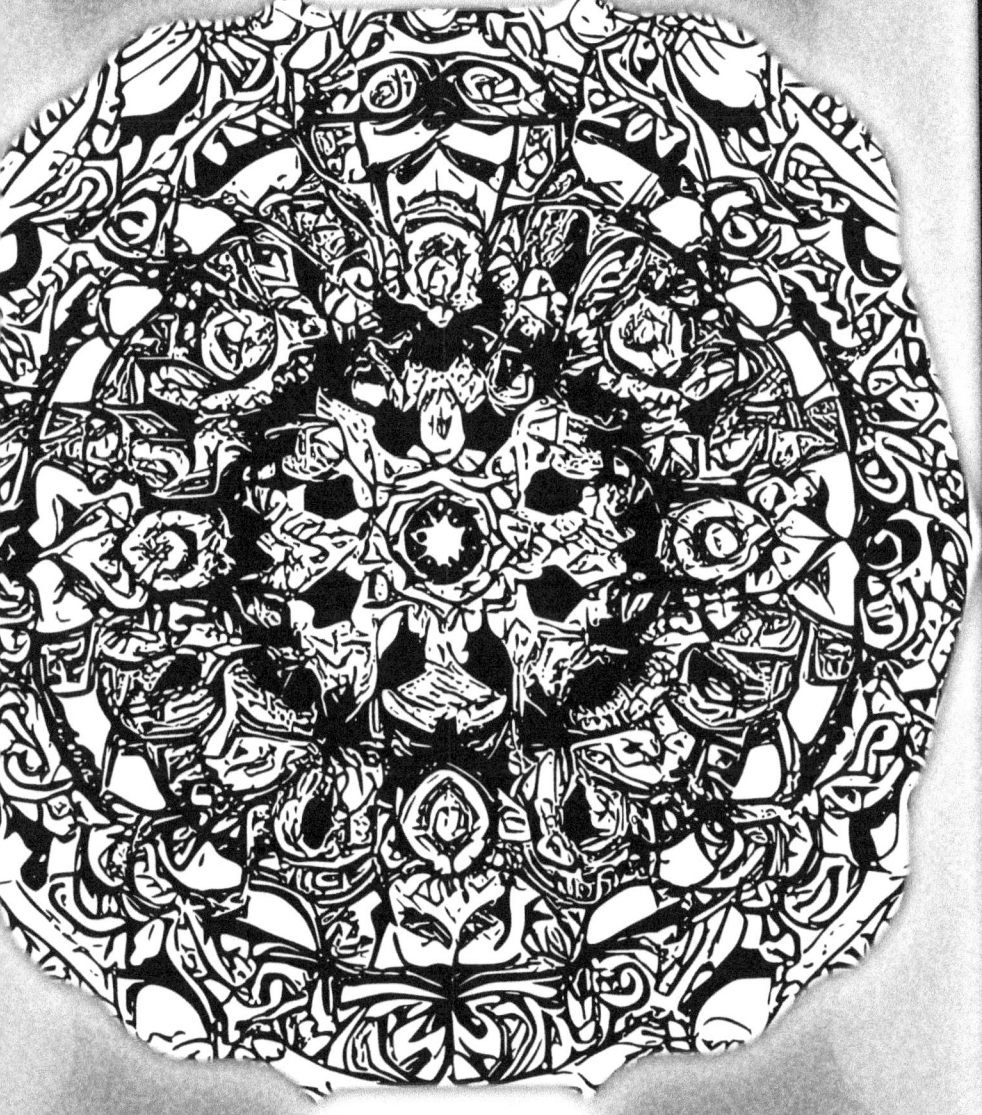

_____

Artist's name

_____

Date

Mandala

TRIP

CHAPTER · 1

XVII

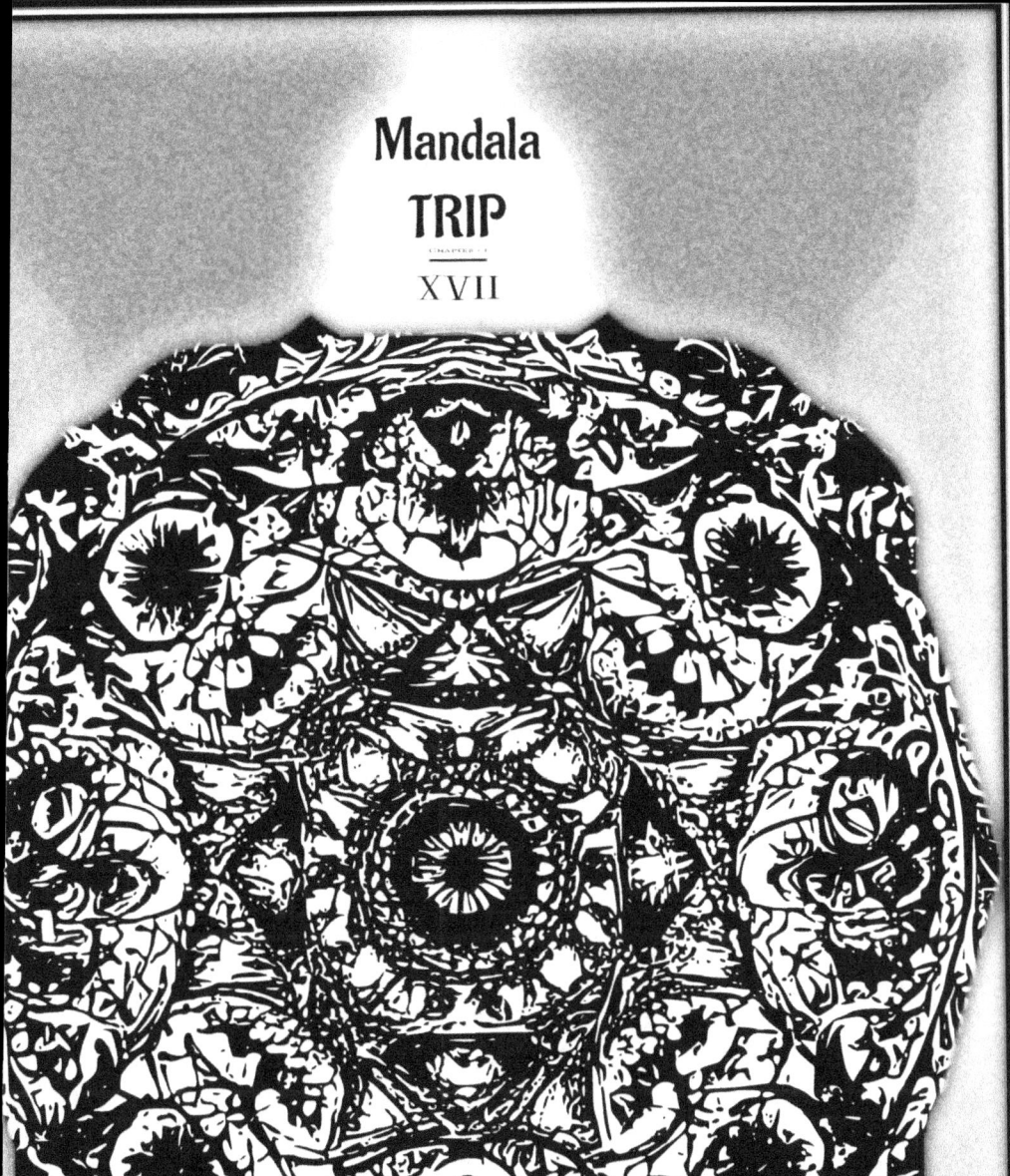

Mandala
TRIP
CHAPTER - I
XVIII

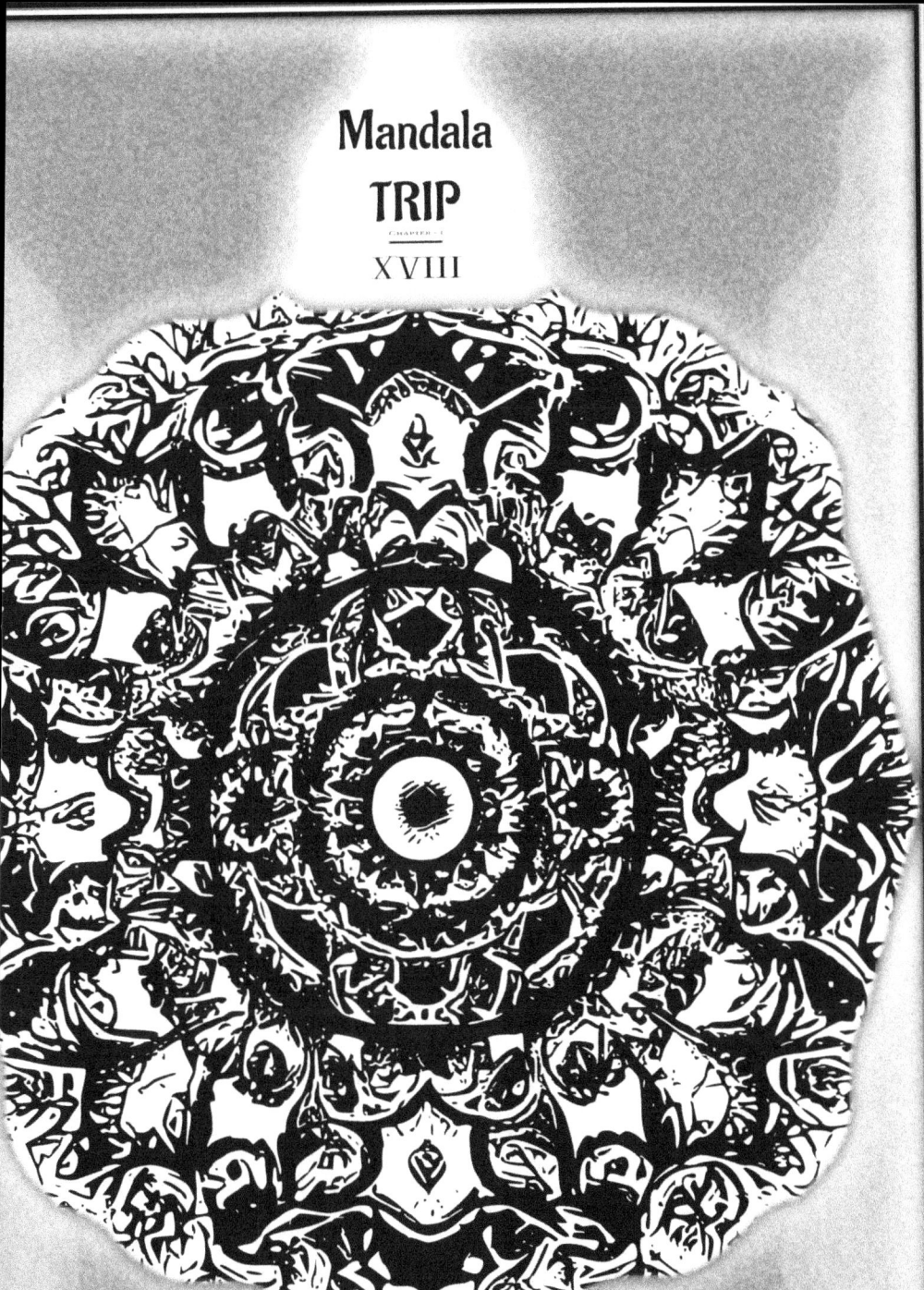

Artist's name

Date

Mandala
TRIP

CHAPTER·1

XIX

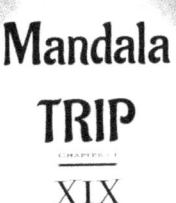

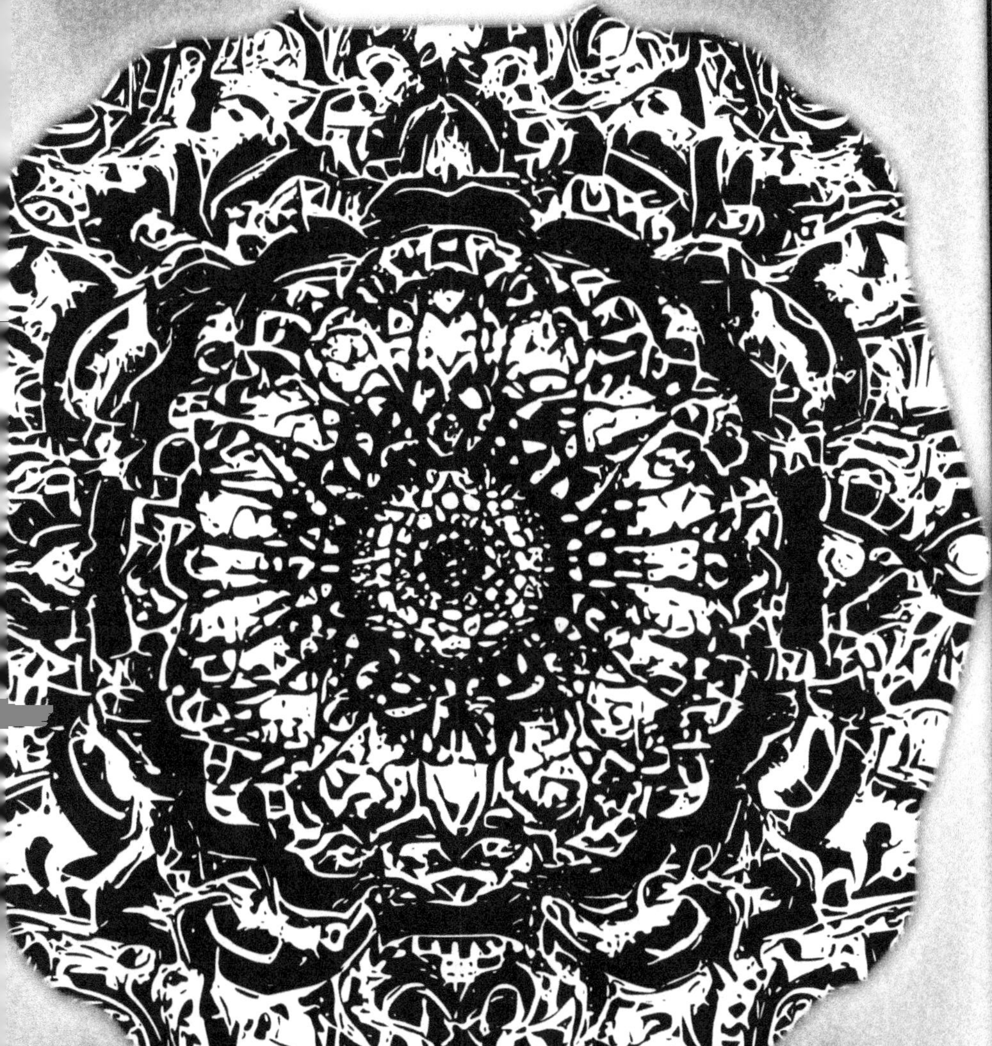

Artist's name

Date

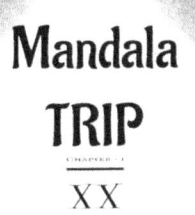

Mandala
TRIP
CHAPTER 1
XX

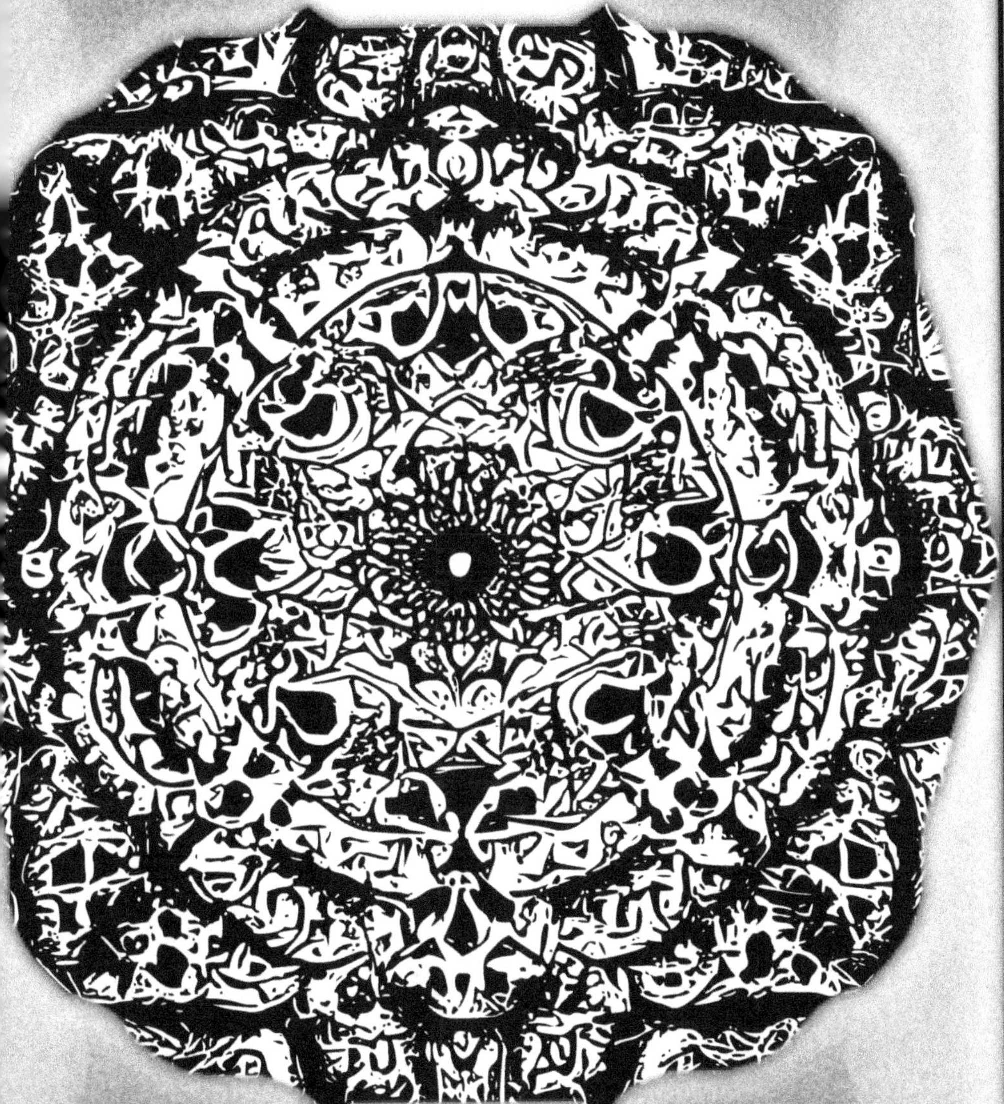

Artist's name

Date

Mandala

TRIP

CHAPTER · I

XXI

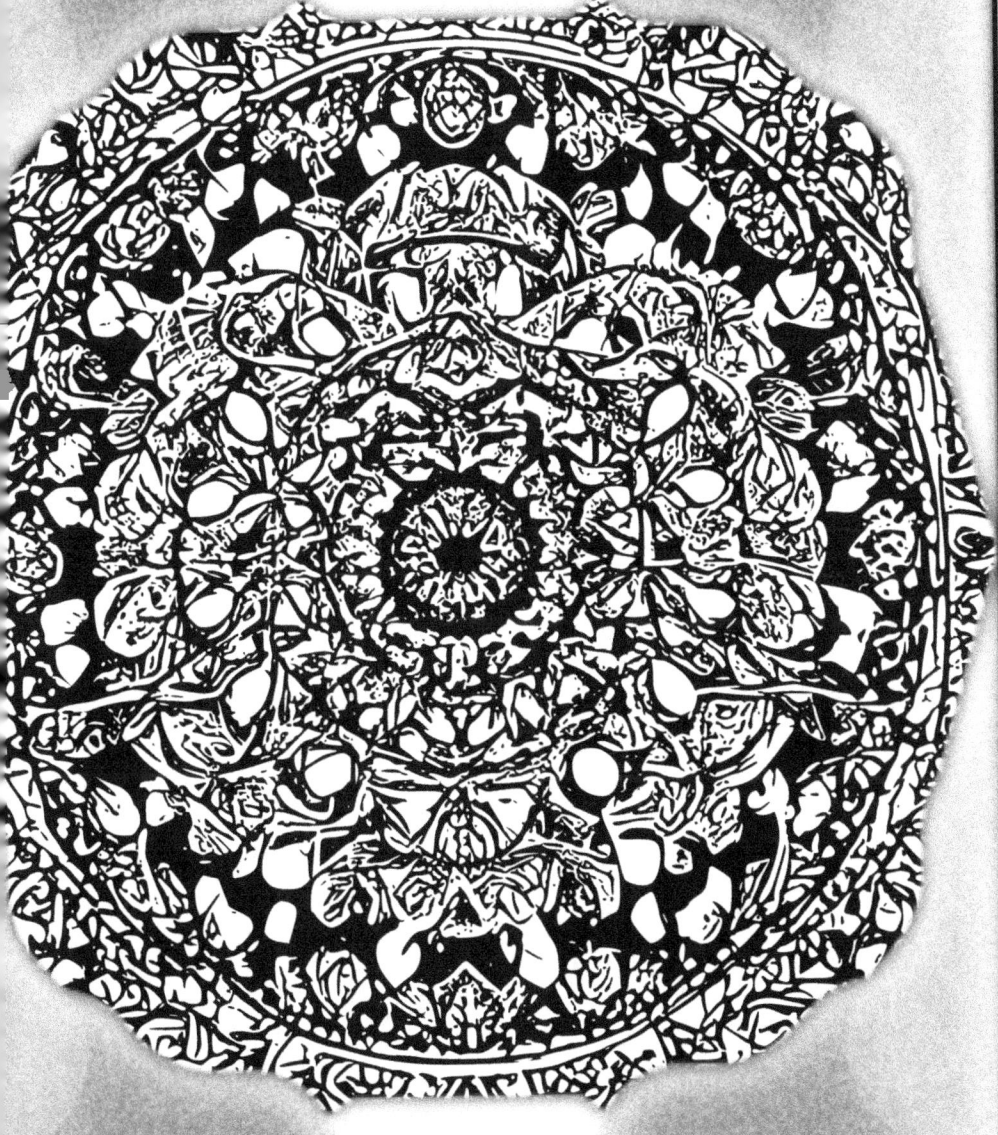

Artist's name

Date

Mandala

TRIP

CHAPTER · I

XXII

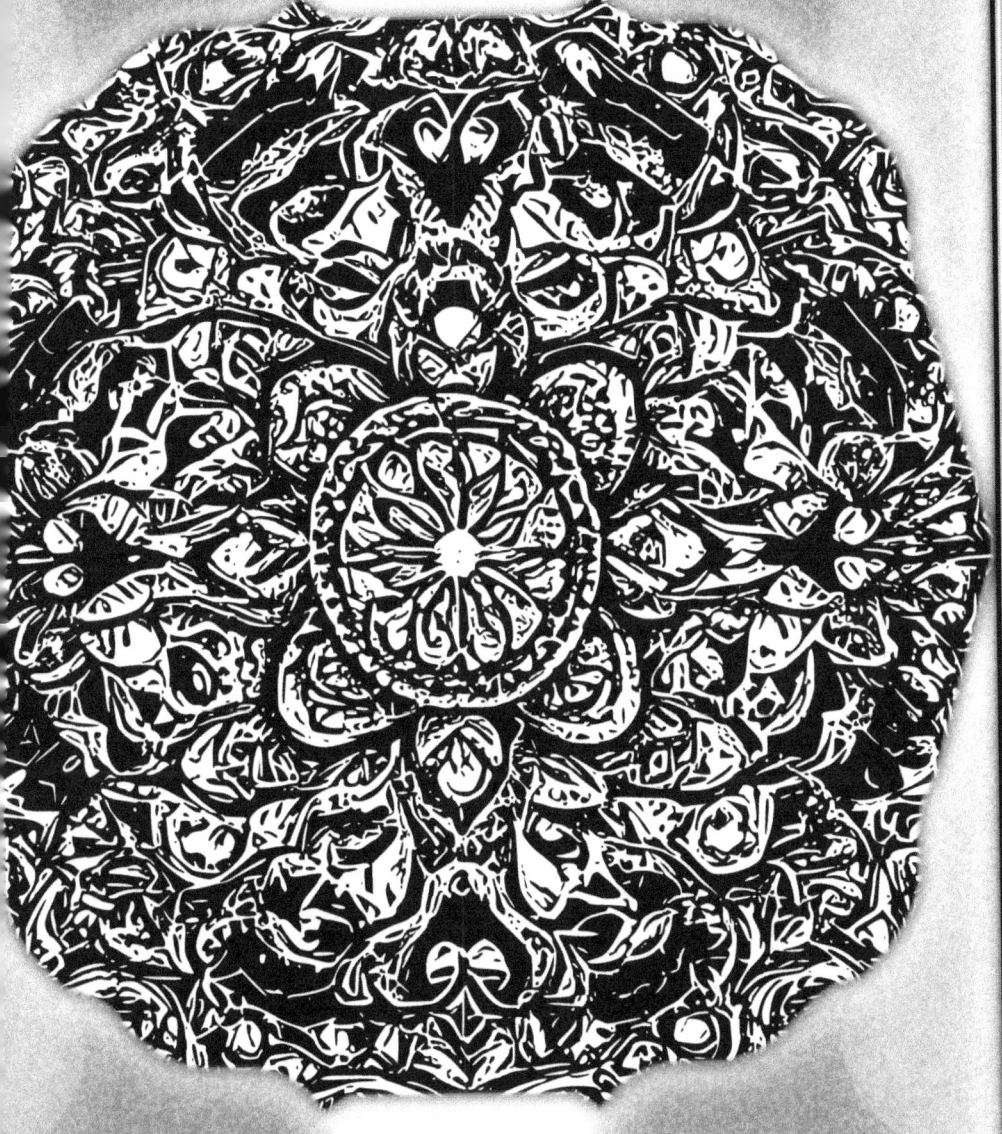

Artist's name

Date

Mandala
TRIP
CHAPTER
XXIII

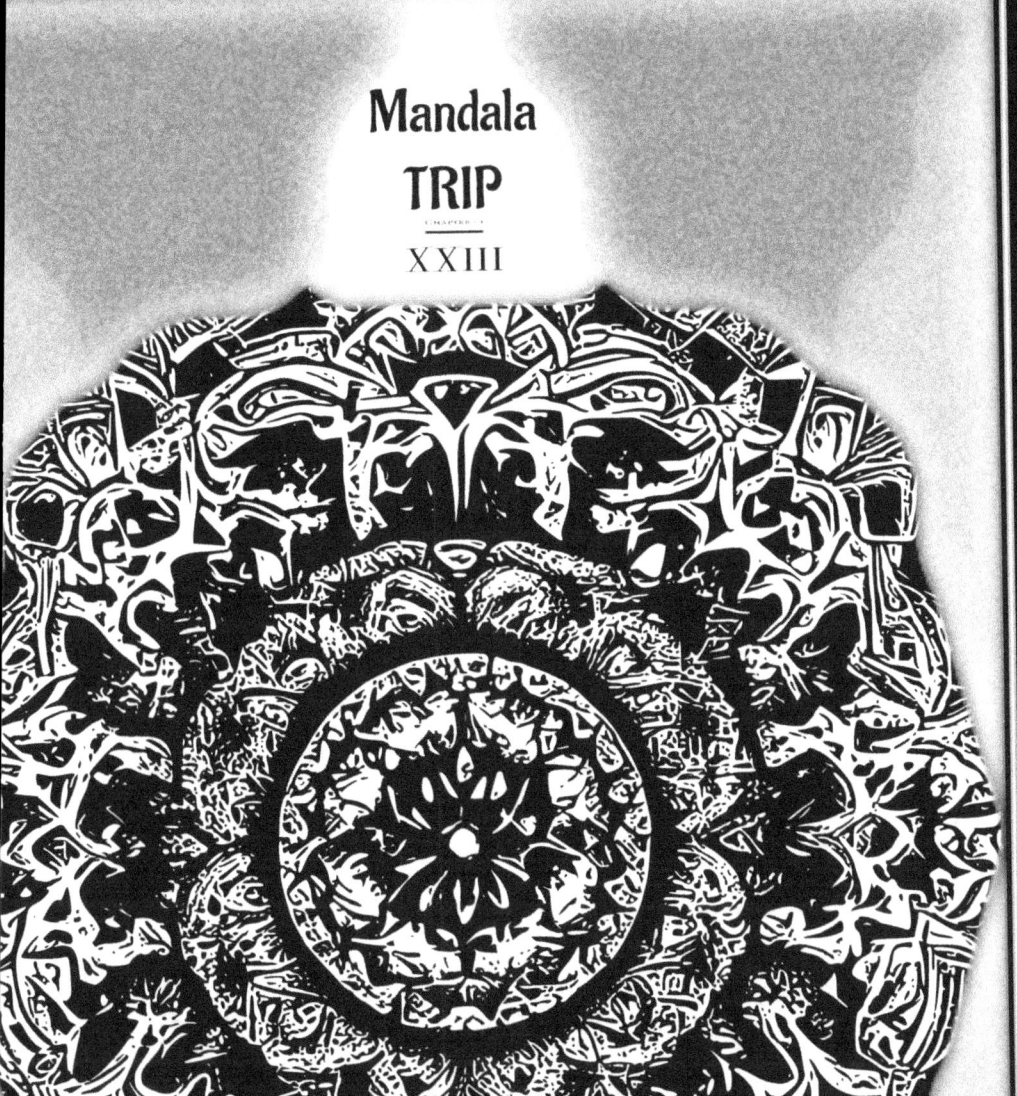

Artist's name

Date

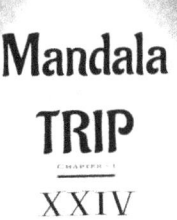

Mandala
TRIP
CHAPTER - 1
XXIV

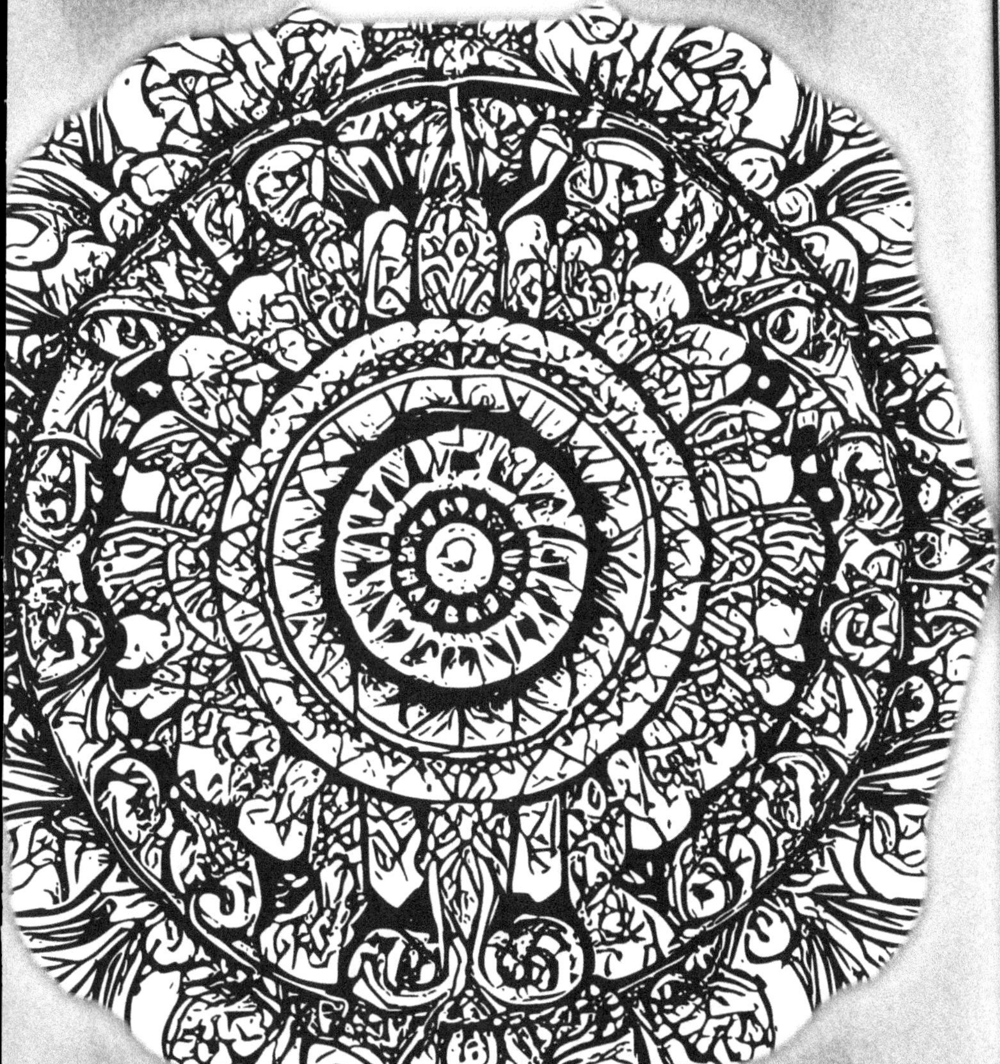

Artist's name

Date

Mandala
TRIP
CHAPTER I
XXV

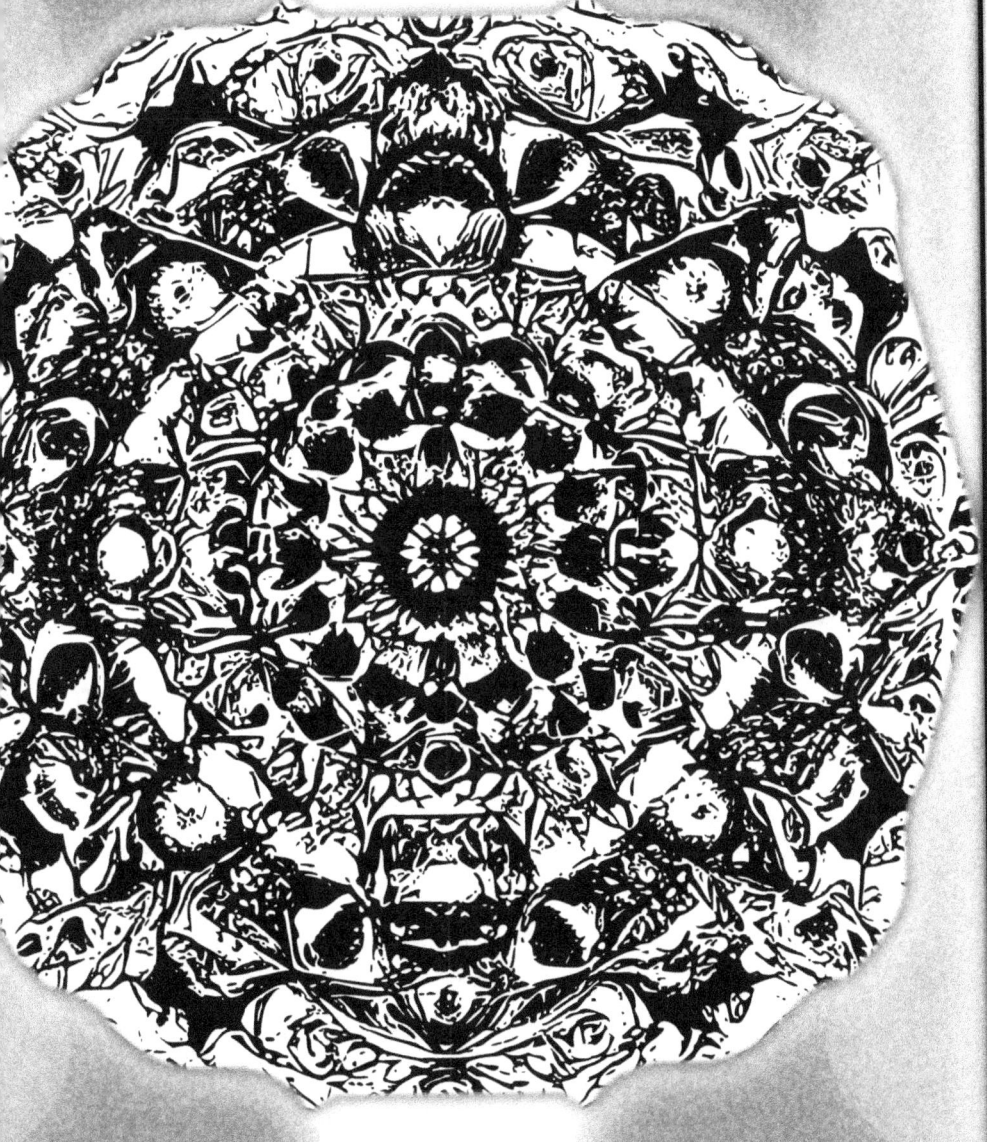

Artist's name

Date